Ten Weeks

MW00769382

A Practical Program for Singers of All Levels

By Kristin King

Kristin L. King

Copyright 2014 Kristin King

Contents

Introduction

What you hold in your hands is a manual on the basics of vocal technique. It doesn't matter if you haven't had formal training with a vocal coach or if you've spent thousands of hours (and dollars) studying music. Maybe you want to sing for yourself or your family, or perhaps you want to share your talent in a community or church choir, or you'd like to learn to sing more professionally. If you desire to acquire more knowledge on singing and want to know how to do it right, every time, this book is for you!

Singing is definitely an art form and can be quite abstract. Many people don't realize that singing is also a science. It's not an exact science, because each person's singing voice varies because of his or her unique vocal cords, but there are certain measures that anyone can physically take to improve his or her singing. For instance, if you want to develop a more consistent tone every time you perform, you can learn the correct way to breathe and use it each time you sing. If you want to strengthen your chest voice, this book will show you the correct way to engage your diaphragm, your "singing muscle," to give you the support that you need to croon those beautiful notes.

Business entrepreneur Martha Stewart says you should write the book you'd want to read. I've read some fine material on singing, but I am consistently disappointed by the lack of material written for the singer who needs and wants to learn the basics. As a result of this need, I wrote this book, inspired by my many voice students who have expressed their desire to learn more about the art of singing and how to improve their own practice.

I have been singing since my first church solo at the age of three. I can't ever remember falling in love with singing, because it was something I just did. It is as natural to me as breathing. Therefore, I spent my primary and secondary school years performing as often as I could in church and on stage. It made perfect sense to study singing in college, as it was the true love of my life. In 2006, I graduated with a four-year bachelor's degree in vocal performance.

Even though I had learned much about my own voice, I wouldn't start my in-depth practice of vocal techniques until I formed my company, Kristin King Music, in 2008. That is when I began teaching voice and piano lessons, and I started to fully realize how to utilize practical vocal singing methods with my students. I never preach anything that I don't practice myself. I sing almost every Sunday morning for several hours at my church, and people are often amazed that I still have a singing voice after hours of use. However, I never miss the opportunity to warm-up, and I believe that is the sole reason I rarely get laryngitis. In fact, as a result of using the strategies you will soon learn in this book, I believe my voice has become stronger and richer since I graduated from college.

How to Use This Book

The purpose of this book is to provide you with the tools to get you singing correctly with confidence, even if you can't afford a vocal coach. Of course, I recommend that if you would like to continue your study of voice, you find a skilled teacher in your area. However, wouldn't it be nice to go to your first lesson with a general knowledge of how the voice works and how to use your different ranges?

This book is meant to function as a ten-week program that anyone who wants to develop a better singing voice can work through in two-and-a-half months. There are several ways to work through it. If you wish, you can read the entire book to get an overview of the tips and techniques presented within. Then you can go back and work through a chapter each week until you've worked through all ten weeks and focused on the chapter-specific content. Alternatively, you can simply start at week one and work through a chapter each week.

The chapters should be read and used sequentially as they build on one another and culminate in a performance at the end of week ten. Once you have completed the program, you should notice marked improvement in your singing. At that point, you may wish to begin study with a voice teacher, or, if you like, you can work through the program again starting with week one. It will not hamper your singing to do so, but will improve it as you gain more knowledge about your voice.

I hope you enjoy every minute of your singing journey! If you wish to become a better singer and seek to understand how you sing, you now have the power and the means to do so! Here's to building your better voice, the smart way!

Happy Singing,

Kristin King

First Things First

Singing Terms You Absolutely Need to Know!

Belting—forcing a loud tone in the mid to upper register; without proper technique, belting can be deteriorating to vocal health

Breaks—places in the voice where the singer naturally flows from chest to head voice tones, head to falsetto tones (for males), and back down

Breath support—the air behind the sound that allows you to correctly and comfortably sing a pitched note

Chest voice—a deep piercing register, often considered "full-voice" singing that is highly popular in commercial music styles

Classical music—"operatic" style of music that largely relies on head voice and vibrato techniques

Commercial music—style of music that encompasses popular music genres (pop, rock, country, contemporary Christian, jazz, et cetera) and has its own unique vocal techniques; does not include classical music

Diaphragm—the muscle located at the base of the ribs that aids in breathing, your "singing muscle"; use it and the sky's the limit! Forget to use it, and you're likely to run out of air to produce a quality sound

Falsetto—same as the head voice for a woman; the top register of notes for both male and female voices; characterized by a childish, crying sound

Hard palate—the roof of the mouth

Head voice—the upper register of the voice that generally yields quieter, less powerful notes if the vibrato is not supported or well-developed

Mixed voice—the joining of the chest and head voice to create a very pleasant mix, especially on higher notes

Passaggio—the divide or break between the chest and head voice, falls on the note Ab (black key on the piano between G and A)

Pitch—perceived frequency of sound; for vocal purposes, a singer can be under the pitch (flat), above the pitch (sharp), or right on the pitch (the sweet spot!)

Range—the span of the absolute lowest to absolute highest note that a voice can produce

Soft palate—the soft, muscular area at the back of the throat; when used correctly can aid in a deep, rich singing tone; incorrectly can restrict the sound and cause a thin, undesirable tone

Tone—the quality of sound that a particular voice produces; can be warm, bright, dark, et cetera

Tongue—aids in formation of words during singing, but can also be the source of tension that prevents good tone for many singers

Vibrato—oscillating up and down around a certain pitch; correct vibrato should originate from the diaphragm

Vocal cords—also known as vocal folds, located in the larynx; vibrate when air hits them and helps to produce a sound

Week One: Getting Started

So, you want to sing? Maybe you already love to
sing and get the chance to perform often in front
of many people, or at least you sing in your
shower getting ready for work in the morning.
Either way, singing is a wonderful way to express
your musicality, and it's even more wonderful
when you know how to sing correctly. Believe it
or not, if you want to sing now and keep singing
all your life, you must learn to sing correctly or
you can actually do permanent damage to your
voice and your vocal cords. Let's be honest: a
vocal "fry" isn't the most pleasant sound in the
world. It's also not pleasant to have a scope put
down your throat by a doctor to determine how
many nodes have formed on your cords.

There is a surefire way to stay away from the "fry" and unpleasant nodules. That is by practicing your singing while using correct techniques every time. Don't worry if you don't know what those are just yet. By the end of our ten weeks together, you should have a good idea of how to take care of your vocal instrument for the rest of your life.

The most important thing about singing you must remember is this:

Singing should never hurt!

That's right; it should not cause you any physical pain in your throat, nose, or any other body part when you sing correctly. At the first sign of any pain or discomfort, stop singing and readjust your posture and/or tone until it no longer hurts. Overlooking or ignoring discomfort when you are singing can often lead to more major vocal problems. So, don't sing if it hurts—simple as that!

Now let's look at exactly how the body produces a sound or musical tone. I promise I won't bore you with too much biology, but at the very least, you need to understand how the body works to produce a tone. This will also help you recognize what's going on with your body and appreciate how you can create such incredible sounds.

Every sound you make starts with a breath. You must have adequate air to produce an adequate sound. When you engage your diaphragm (a muscle in your chest that aids in breathing), the lungs pump air up to the vocal cords (also known as the vocal folds), which then vibrate and form an audible pitch. Then the articulators (the tongue, soft and hard palates, cheeks, and lips) shape the sound as it flows from the mouth. This is how a single sound is produced every time. Now you can see how inadequate breath support will fail to produce the desired tone in singing. If you were to take a shallow breath, not engaging the diaphragm, your vocal cords would not have enough air to produce a quality sound. Then you might try to "help" yourself by tensing the neck or lifting the tongue. This type of singing, occurring repeatedly, would eventually cause you to lose your voice, because your throat is not meant to take on the work of your diaphragm.

The vocal cords are located in the larynx in your throat. The size of the vocal cords determines the range of pitches that a person can sing. The size also varies, depending if you're male or female, with men having deeper voices because of deeper, thicker folds. Your genetics and gender determine which voice part you can comfortably sing.

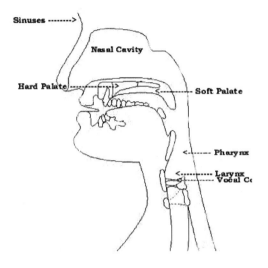

Illustration courtesy of www.asharpmusic.com.

Many vocal problems originate from a lack of
sufficient air. Also, not engaging the diaphragm
(underneath the ribs) to support the sound can
force unnecessary tension on the throat and cause
problems. Short-term, you might finish singing a
song with a sore throat. Long-term, you can
develop nodes on the cords, which are hard knots
of tissue that develop from improper vocal use.

New York University Langone Medical Center states, "nodules form on the vocal cords . . . associated with yelling, screaming or improper voice use. Singer's nodules are frequently found in amateur singers, and may be due to improper singing technique."[1]

These are the types of problems that you should seek to avoid. Unfortunately, a doctor cannot see nodes without the aid of a scope down your throat (which, in my opinion, is no fun). So, let's avoid those altogether by taking care of our voices as best we can.

Here are several tips to remember when caring for your singing voice.

1. Stop if it hurts! If you're singing a song and you start to feel discomfort, stop if you are able to. If not, finish the song, then rest the voice and examine possible reasons for the pain. Are you fully engaging the diaphragm (easily done by pulling in the abdominal muscles)? Are your throat, tongue, or lips taking on any unnecessary tension when you sing? Try to find the root of the pain and that will usually help you figure out the solution.

2. Be sure to hydrate properly. Hydration is key when caring for your cords! The best hydration is water, because your body needs this fluid anyway. Your cords must be properly lubricated to vibrate optimally. Room temperature water is ideal. Cold water can be shocking to your throat and cords if you down it moments before you sing. Another beverage I recommend for a scratchy throat is decaffeinated hot tea (any flavor) with a little honey. Avoid drinking dairy products, such as milk, before singing as this coats the throat and makes it more difficult to sing.

3. No smoking! This should be a given, but when I was in college, there were people all around me majoring in vocal performance and lighting up every chance they got! Smoking and singing are like eating a huge hamburger and fries while working out. It's completely ridiculous and counterproductive! I'm not going to preach to you, but if you really want to sing, smoking of any kind should never be an option.

4. Consider vocal rest. If you've got a big part to sing, or you will be singing for hours at a time in the near future, try to set aside some time beforehand to go on vocal rest. This means not speaking, singing, or making a sound for as much time as possible before it's time to warm up for the big performance. I read in pop singer Celine Dion's autobiography that she has gone on vocal rest for up to two weeks at a time before a big concert tour! This is not to suggest that you have to be silent for two weeks (that would be difficult for most of us!), but even several hours of vocal rest can be beneficial. Just make sure that after coming off your vocal rest, you don't undo all your hard work by immediately overusing your voice. This brings us to the next tip.

5. Always warm-up! We'll talk more about this in the next section, but you need to treat singing as you would a physical workout. You would never walk into the gym and immediately begin bench-pressing a large amount of weight on cold muscles. Likewise, you should never begin any vigorous singing without an adequate warm-up. Warm-up + hard singing = happy cords and happy singers!

I hope this introduction has given you some basic knowledge about how your body works to produce sound, and perhaps you've picked up a practical tip for honing your singing voice. Don't wait to practice these tips; start today! Also, to get the most out of *Ten Weeks to a Better Voice,* be sure to complete the next steps section at the conclusion of each chapter. Next week, I'll be discussing the supreme importance of vocal warm-ups!

Singer's Next Steps

- Read this chapter thoroughly and highlight any terms that may be unclear to you. Research unfamiliar terms, using the glossary at the beginning or by searching online.

- Define your goals for your singing voice, and write them down somewhere you will see them. Review your goals each time you study a chapter in this book, and write down two or three action steps you can work on each week.

- Develop a daily voice workout using the warm-ups provided by a voice instructor or research "voice warm-ups" on YouTube. Choose your favorites and practice them.

Week Two: Getting Ready to Sing

Before every workout, many trainers recommend that you engage in dynamic stretching to avoid soreness and injury to your muscles during and after the workout. Dynamic stretching involves movement, mimicking the movement you'll soon be performing in a sweat-inducing workout. Likewise, before singing, it's imperative for you to warm up your voice to help avoid injury to your vocal cords during long periods of singing. Heavy singing is when you'll be using your full vocal range with full breathing techniques. Light singing can be thought of as simply using your voice to hum or sing in a playful manner for a few minutes without much exertion. Through warm-ups, your voice will gain flexibility, and your range (the span of notes from lowest to highest) will increase as you perform voice exercises on a consistent basis.

Here are some reasons why you should incorporate warm-ups in your vocal routine:

- Warming up gets the body and the cords prepared for heavy singing
- Warming up helps to protect the cords from injury
- Warming up helps you safely and quickly develop agility in your range
- Warming up gets you in the habit of practicing good vocal technique on a regular basis
- Warming up allows you to further develop chest, head, and mixed voice ranges in the healthiest manner possible

Have you ever noticed that when you try to speak or sing loud first thing in the morning without warming up, it feels (and maybe sounds) like slogging through mud? Pitches that would normally be easy to reach cause you strain and limit your range. That's because your voice has been at rest for about eight hours and now you're suddenly attempting to use it to its full capacity. Your vocal cords are saying, "I don't think so!" because they are not created to go from no use to full use without some preparation.

This is why it's so important to warm-up before heavy singing (or speaking). Your voice needs a chance to wake up, just like the rest of your body. Most people aren't able to pop right out of bed the first time the alarm goes off at 5:30 am. If you are like me, you start to ease yourself out of bed with a full-body stretch. If you ease into singing through some gentle vocal warm-ups, your range will reflect it, and you will keep unnecessary tension off the cords. Remember, the goal is to keep you singing healthy now and for the rest of your life. Warm-ups will serve to prolong your voice, as long as you use them often!

Roger Kain, author of *The Complete Vocal Workout*, comments that, "Exercises [warm-ups] are targeted at problem solving in a way that songs are not . . . Exercises should . . . stretch you . . . [and] they should build up good habits so that your technique becomes automatic. In other words, exercises help you to cope with your voice under any circumstance. Whatever your problem, there's an exercise to solve it."[2]

Like regular exercise, you will need to develop a vocal warm-up routine in order to see the desired results you wish to achieve. That means that warming up once a week isn't going to do much for your voice. Shaping your voice into what you want it to be is going to cost some time and effort. The recommended schedule for voice training is three to four days a week for thirty minutes to an hour. Also be aware that overworking your voice (singing or warming up too much) can be just as harmful as underworking it. The idea is to find the right balance!

Stretching other parts of your body, just as you would do before aerobic exercise, can also help prepare you for singing. Give this series of full-body stretches a try before launching into your daily voice work.

1. Stand with a neutral posture—not too tall, but neither slumped over. Feet should be about shoulder-width apart, hands should be comfortably at your side, and your chest should be slightly lifted.

2. While inhaling deeply, raise your arms around in a circle and bring them above your head. Stop the breath when your hands are reaching toward the ceiling.

3. Exhale slowly as your hands float back to their starting position (Note: You want to hear yourself inhale and exhale on this exercise, because the purpose is to focus on your breathing). Perform steps 1–3 several more times until you feel relaxed. Make sure that you are breathing deeply, especially by the third or fourth breath. Feel any tension fade from your body.

4. Raise arms to tabletop position (arms and elbows parallel to the floor) and twist side to side from the waist, keeping the feet firmly planted on the ground. Keep doing this movement as you feel your abdominals engage and tighten.

5. Stand again in neutral posture and this time exhale slowly as you bend over, exhaling all the air from the body. Inhale and slowly lift back up to neutral position. Repeat this movement several times. By ringing all the air out of the body and then taking it in again, you may feel light-headed. This is ok and is normal at first!

6. Do several shoulder rolls—forward first and then reverse. Do several gentle neck rolls, being careful not to pop the neck.

7. Now take several deep yawns, but pitch them. Begin high and allow the pitch to float down as you say "haaaaaaaaaaaa."

You should feel loose and ready to begin the vocal exercises after these stretches. Now is a great time to run through three or four vocal exercises that you can comfortably sing. Remember as you sing through them that you are warming up the voice. Your voice should be light and airy. Don't get upset if you make a mistake. Just find your place and continue. Vocal exercises are for practicing technique; they don't have to (and shouldn't) be perfect! Just be consistent with them and you will see results.

If your throat starts to feel sore, make sure you aren't over-singing. Relax your articulators (tongue, cheeks, lips, hard and soft palates) and make sure none of these is causing you unnecessary tension. Remember that correct singing should never hurt. If you are just starting this vocal workout and have never done it consistently before, you may experience initial tiredness of the voice, but that is completely normal, and it will subside as you practice on a regular schedule. Remember, it should not hurt!

This is my recommendation for your vocal schedule on those three or four days you set aside to do a vocal workout: Start with the stretches described above to prepare your entire body to sing. Then use some selected vocal exercises (provided by a vocal instructor or search YouTube for "vocal exercises") and sing lightly through each exercise, spending about 15–20 minutes total on the warm-up. At this point, your voice should feel ready to fully sing, and you can safely rehearse your vocal material. Try to choose songs that are demanding and utilize the techniques of your warm-ups. Spend about 20 minutes working through your material and jot down any voice problems you may experience on certain phrases, notes, or words. It's a great idea to have a sheet of lyrics for the song(s) you are working on, so you can make notes for future use. After you finish working on your material, you can always perform or repeat a warm-up exercise as a cool down if you wish.

The true purpose of warm-ups is to help you work out vocal problems before you perform whatever material you are working on. I promise, if you are consistent to stick with your vocal routine and you utilize the warm-ups provided, you will gain a stronger voice in no time!

Singer's Next Steps

- Read this chapter and try the stretches before your next vocal workout.

- Go to YouTube and search for vocal exercises. Choose three or four new ones to work on throughout the week.

- Look at your schedule for the next week and pencil in a time to practice vocal workouts for three to four of those days. Stick to your routine this week and make note of your progress. Did the vocal exercises get easier? Did your range increase? How did your voice sound on your personal material after you warmed up?

Week Three: Technical Preparation

I had this lovely dream when I was a child about the kind of house I wanted to live in when I grew up. I remember sitting in the backseat of my parents' car and looking at different houses that were for sale. I didn't think about bedrooms, kitchens, or living spaces. My primary question was, "How would a piano look in this house?" If I couldn't picture a baby grand piano in the house, I knew I could never live there!

That dream of having a music room never went away. In fact, when my husband and I moved into our home, the very first piece of furniture that was delivered was my wedding present: a beautiful ebony baby grand piano. I remember positioning the piano in my music room and sitting down to play it, the tones echoing throughout an otherwise empty house.

The point of this little story is that I needed a space in which to be creative. We were lucky enough to find a home that provided a bonus space that made a wonderful music room. As you go about preparing to gain a better singing voice, you too will need a space in which to practice. This does not have to be an entire room dedicated to your hobby of singing. It can be a small space in your office, or a comfy chair in your living room next to a bookshelf that houses your music collection. If you can dedicate a place that is all your own to practice your art, you will probably be much more inclined to return there often. It's like your own personal sanctuary. If you have a spouse and/or children, it might be a good idea to establish a time with them that you will be "occupied" in your space, working on your music. It could be for thirty minutes at a time that you ask to not be disturbed. Not only will you be getting some valuable alone time, but you will also establish a productive routine during those precious minutes.

Tools for Singing

Great news! You have carved out a space for your singing and are ready to get started with your new vocal habits. Now you just need a couple of items to be on your way.

The first two items I recommend are a blank journal or notebook and a pencil. Being that I am a musician, I like to track my progress in singing using a journal-like dating style. After I have completed a vocal session, I open to a blank page in my journal, jot down the date, and detail my progress. I also use the same journal for notes and progress with my voice students. I list any ideas I have for new songs or material that I've recently heard that might make good performance material.

And, of course, I jot down any new musical concepts or ideas I come across. I actually wrote the majority of this book in my music journal before I ever typed it on the computer.

Your journal can be laid out in any style you prefer. The important part is that you have a place to track your progress in a manner that works for you. I recommend using pencil because it's erasable. If you have music that you are borrowing or wish to make notes on, it's a lot easier to clean up when you use pencil.

Use your journal to record the goals you've set as you work through *Ten Weeks to a Better Voice.* Get specific about your problem areas and what you want to improve. Do you want to have more confidence when you sing higher? Jot it down. As you work through specific exercises and songs, make note of the ones that increase your confidence. If you're constantly on the lookout for new material to sing, why not start a page dedicated to songs you hear that you might be interested in trying to tackle.

With the journal or notebook, the sky's the limit. This is your personal study of your voice and you have to do what works best for you.

Other materials that are helpful to have as you begin preparation for singing could include a CD player, MP3 player, or computer and a set of speakers. When you are first practicing a new vocal exercise or a song, I highly recommend singing along with the recording. As you progress and learn the nuances of that particular song, you can search for a track online that removes the singer's voice so you can practice by yourself and follow your growth.

As you dive into your material, make learning gains, and discover a world of possibilities with your voice, you may even wish to purchase a keyboard or piano for your music space. Don't know how to play the piano? Invest in a few piano lessons, so you can learn the notes of the keyboard and learn to decipher what key(s) you sing best in. Obviously, this is an optional step, but many people who study voice find that it's helpful to know something about the basics of piano playing and that it greatly enhances their progress with singing.

Ok, you have gathered your materials and are now ready to get down to business about bettering your singing voice. Before we get technical, there is one last thing you need to do. Grab your planner, Palm Pilot, Blackberry, or e-Calendar and look at the next ten weeks. I want you to come up with a schedule that allows you to carve out three to four thirty-minute sessions a week of uninterrupted voice time. That's roughly one-and-a-half to two hours per week dedicated to the art of singing. Trust me, the time will fly, but you probably won't create the time to practice, if you don't schedule it.

If it's not in your calendar, something else will suddenly look appealing when it's time to have your vocal practice! However, if you have a standing appointment with yourself, you are much more likely to show up and get it done!

Discovering Your Range

Are you an alto, tenor, bass, or soprano? If you don't know, don't panic. This is where you will seek the help of a professional voice teacher and ask them if they will "voice you." Voice teachers can be found in a variety of places, but if you don't know where to find one, ask other singers you know for recommendations or do an Internet search for voice teachers in your area. Once you've found one, ask him or her for one meeting to help you find your range. Many teachers will gladly do this free of charge, especially if you might bring them future business. The voice teacher will run you through a series of exercises that help to determine your range and which voice part you are naturally the most comfortable singing. Please remember that even if you are an alto or bass, it does not automatically mean you will be singing alto or bass songs the rest of your life. This is only a starting point, a springboard, if you will. You want to find out as much information about your voice as possible, before you push yourself to the limit and begin to expand your singing. Knowing what range you comfortably sing will help you determine your long-term goals for expanding the voice. It will also give you a place to start. If you voice as a soprano, starting your vocal journey with a lower, belty-type song would not be the wisest choice. Sure, you may love the song, but it needs to serve as a goal for you, not the first song you would choose to learn.

After you are voiced, be sure to ask the vocal coach if there are any good starting exercises or songs that you can work on. He or she may open your mind to a world of possibilities you never thought about before.

Now that you have the tools in your arsenal and you know your primary voice part, it's time to dive into the deep waters of singing! Next up: it's all about the head voice.

Singer's Next Steps

- Have you carved out a space for your singing? If not, stop reading right now and designate a place to work on your craft! Why not make a sign that says "Do Not Disturb: Working on My Dream." Use it any time you are working on your singing.

- Start a singing journal and write down your goals for the next ten weeks. Now look at the top three goals you would like to accomplish. Highlight them. These are going to be the primary areas of focus that guide your singing for the next two-and-a-half months.

- Contact a voice teacher or skilled musician and ask to be voiced, if you are unsure. Voicing you should only take a matter of minutes, but is extremely necessary for you to be successful at this process.

- Start a page in your journal to list appropriate vocal exercises and the names of the songs you will be working on during the next few weeks.

Week Four: Strengthening the Head Voice

Chances are, you've been to a concert, show, or church service and have heard a man or woman sing with an upper range that seems endless. Each unbelievably high note is perfectly pitched and haunting. With the singer's natural amplification, a microphone seems and is, in fact, optional. I am here to tell you that you too can sing like this with all the power you have to hit those sweet, sweet high notes. And it doesn't matter if you're an alto, bass, or baritone. You don't have to be a soprano or tenor to develop an incredibly strong head range. Your voice part is just the part you are most comfortable singing. It doesn't mean you can't expand your range, if you desire and commit to the time and effort it takes to develop these notes.

This is where classical training for singers is the most helpful. Classical music relies heavily on vibrato and using the natural head voice to amplify the tone. Many classical vocal pieces will expand your head range further than some commercial pieces because they employ many high notes. Classical voice teachers will work with their students first on developing the flexibility of high notes in the head voice, because this technique is absolutely critical to singing the classical style of music.

While I am not a classical teacher, nor do I profess to be a classical singer, I greatly admire singers of this genre, because I know they are properly trained to use the agility in their voices to sing those beautiful high notes. Therefore, I begin the study of different voice ranges by starting with the head voice.

If you will take the time to develop a strong head voice range,

the other ranges of the voice (chest and mid-range/mixed)

will grow stronger naturally!

Not that you won't work on the other parts of the voices, because you will, but working the head voice range is like killing three birds with one stone. One stronger range naturally makes the other two stronger also. This is why: once you learn proper head voice singing techniques, you will automatically be using correct breath support, which will aid in reaching other notes that are low or loud or both. It takes concentrated breath support to reach those high notes and even more breath to hold them; therefore, singing high is truly a full-body activity. Your throat will not be able to croak out those high C's without a strong diaphragm underneath it in action.

So just how do you find your head voice and know that you are using it instead of chest or mix voice? Typically, notes that you sing in this range feel as if they are resonating out of the top your head as opposed to your chest. One vocal teacher describes the different ranges as a four-story building. To illustrate:

4th floor—Penthouse Whistle tones/ falsetto
3rd floor—Head Range
2nd floor—Mid or Mixed Range
1st floor—Chest Range

Think of your breath support as the elevator that carries you up to each "floor," which represents the different ranges. You are going to need more controlled breath support the higher you go, especially on the whistle tones, which few of us have been blessed with naturally (think singer Mariah Carey).

You can train your voice to sing as high as you wish. It will not happen overnight, but in time, with careful, controlled exercises, you can and will expand your range if you go about it in the right way. In *Vocal Workouts for the Contemporary Singer,* author Anne Peckham says, "Think of your head register as the mother of your entire voice. If it is strong, it will nurture your entire range. Even if your head voice is weak at first, it will become stronger with use."[3]

When it comes to developing a stronger voice overall, it's best to concentrate your effort now on strengthening the head voice. We will take a detailed look at the other ranges too, but I guarantee you will hear the improvement in your voice as you work through head range exercises and songs that challenge you. Many vocal workouts are geared to help you practice strengthening your head voice, but you should also work on finding songs that are just a bit higher than you might usually sing.

Run through a high vocal exercise first and make a note on the music of the pitches you can't reach. Each day that you practice, try to reach higher notes, but make sure you're using proper breath support and stop immediately if you feel any discomfort or strain. Your range will gradually expand as you perform head voice exercises. Then, when working on your actual material, try to emulate the singer's use of vowels and consonants. Notice how the singer shapes his/her vowels on the higher notes. Does the singer sing the higher notes louder or softer? How does he/she approach head voice notes? These are all questions you should be asking as you listen. Then try to copy the singer as closely as you can. Write down your findings in your journal.

If you are practicing in head voice and experience difficulties, here are a few tips:

- Remember that practice makes perfect. Your voice changes from day to day, so you may just be having an "off" day. Don't worry; it happens to all of us! Put your music away and come back to it tomorrow.

- Are you singing a closed or open vowel? Singing a closed vowel will often cause the soft palate to fall, which will strain the pitch. It's completely acceptable to change the vowel to something more open while you are practicing. Once your body has memorized the proper technique, gradually switch back to the original vowel, and it should feel more natural and open to sing.

- Many times, singers approach high notes from underneath the pitch, which makes the desired pitch flat. Try the opposite approach and pretend you are sliding down from a higher pitch to the desired pitch.

- Change your mental mindset. The mind will tell you all sorts of lies if you allow it to, like the following: "You can't hit that note! Only first sopranos and tenors can hit that note." Or, "You will never get this; you might as well quit it now." No, no, no! Remember to "take captive every thought to make it obedient to Christ" (2 Corinthians 10:5[4]). God would never talk to you like that because he sees you as fearfully and wonderfully made. Therefore, don't ever give up! See yourself as succeeding and you will!

This week, your goal is to focus on strengthening your head voice. In subsequent weeks, you will start your warm-ups by training the head voice first, then gradually train the chest and mixed range. However, if you start with the hard work, your voice will eventually reward you, as you start to notice more freedom in your upper range. Let go of the preconceived notion that you can't sing beyond a certain pitch and just go for it! I bet you'll surprise yourself!

Singer's Next Steps

- Go through specific vocal exercises that strengthen the head voice (search "head voice exercises" on the Internet). Head voice exercises typically take you higher than the normal range of singing. As long as they don't hurt, it's fine to practice head voice exercises that take you out of your comfort zone. Note any problems you are having and see if you can improve your range by singing higher and higher each time.

- Study a classical singer who uses primarily his/ her head voice (some singers to get you started: Josh Groban, Sarah Brightman, Andrea Bocelli, and Luciano Pavarotti). Listen through a particular song several times and make note of how the singer approaches high notes. Try to copy the singer during your own vocal practice.

- Challenge yourself by warming up with two to three high vocal exercises, and then choose a song selection to learn from the singer you studied above. Sing this song through once every three to four days each week and note your progress and ease, particularly on the high notes at the end of one month.

Week Five: Discovering and Developing the Chest Voice

By now, you've been working about a month on developing agility in your range, singing from the diaphragm, and hitting those sweet high notes. Now that your head range is more developed, it's time to start working on the chest range. For many people, the chest voice may be easier to properly develop than the head voice, because the range of the chest voice is the natural range of the speaking voice.

To find your true, natural chest voice range, take a moment and speak this phrase: "Hi, my name is _____." Fill in the blank with your name. Don't attempt to speak any special way. Just talk as you would normally, as if you were introducing yourself to someone for the first time. Make a note of where your inflection occurs. Which words occur lower in your range and which words occur higher? When I say this phrase, I notice that my inflection is higher when I say "Hi" and much lower when I say my name. Once you've discovered what words you speak higher and lower, have a voice instructor match those unpitched words as closely as possible to pitched notes on the piano—or you can try it yourself. Here are the pitched notes I got when I "performed" this phrase:

Hi, my name is Kristin. (Ranged from an F down to a middle C.)

These notes reflect the notes that I would sing naturally and easily in chest voice. Your chest voice is defined as the voice you're most comfortable speaking and singing in. Now, just because you may talk a lot, that doesn't mean when you sing in your chest voice, it's going to be perfect, strong, and instantly resonant. Why not?

Your singing voice uses longer tones than your speaking voice does. Think about it. You don't normally speak as slowly as you sing. So, when you sing in chest voice, you must have complete control over the voice in order to produce a sustained and supported deep tone.

Remember all that hard work you've been doing to become aware of your diaphragm? This is especially important as you are learning to sing in chest voice. Your diaphragm is what produces the controlled breath support you need to sing each strong note. In his blog titled "Forever Singing," Thomas Griffin says, "When you fill your diaphragm with the proper amount of air and control it correctly with cord closure, you have the ability to produce that rich and controlled sound."[5] Griffin is referring to the specific way that the vocal cords open and close when you sing in chest voice.

Now, we will get into a discussion about belting. The singing glossary at the beginning of this book identifies belting as "forcing a loud tone in the mid to upper register." In other words, when you are singing in your natural chest voice range, you wouldn't call that belting. Belting is when you force yourself to extend your chest range into the mixed and head range. Many vocal teachers will advise you against belting at all, because it can do so much damage if done incorrectly. However, I believe that if you are careful and you approach belting systematically, it can be a valuable and powerful tool to use in your singing. Plus, it's downright fun to sing in chest voice when you can do it well!

Television show *American Idol* wouldn't be the same without the vocal styles of Kelly Clarkson and Carrie Underwood. Both of these singers have "powerhouse" voices, so to speak; they are able to belt very high and intense notes in their songs.

Let's face it, those amazing high phrases just wouldn't sound as full or powerful if they were sung in head or mixed voice. I guess you could say I'm neither for nor against belting. If you are going to do it, make sure you do it right! You must ensure that you have complete control over the voice and are engaging the diaphragm when belting. If you don't have control, it's best to keep working on belting through vocal exercises until you gain control over the sound you produce when singing this hard. If you're singing a song that goes higher than you are comfortable singing in chest voice, go ahead and let your voice flip into head range. That's perfectly ok, and no one will probably notice anyway.

As you go through this process of really seeking to understand your voice and how it works, you will learn to differentiate between singing in chest voice and singing in head voice. You will learn your limits! This is a good thing. Before, you may have just been singing without a care in the world, and possibly doing damage to your voice in the process by forcing it beyond what it was naturally able to do. But learning to hear and feel the physiological difference among your ranges helps you know what you need to improve. And remember, the vocal ranges are all in a way connected. Last week, I said that if you strengthen your head voice, your chest and mixed voices will automatically be strengthened as well. Now I'll tell you that as you develop your chest voice, your head voice tones are likely to become warmer. This is especially good news for those of us who tend to sing brighter, more childish-sounding notes at the top of our range. Learning to sing correctly in the chest voice will impart some extra power to those head voice notes also.

Here are some specific keys to developing a strong and powerful chest voice:

- Take a deep inhale, pushing the stomach out, then pull in the stomach on your first chest voice notes, and go for it.

- Do warm-ups that feature long sustained notes with open vowels. Some good words to sing include *yaaa* (pretend like you're yawning), *may*, *no*, and *ha*.

- When performing the exercises or working through a song in chest voice, make sure the jaw is completely relaxed, the soft palate is lifted, your tongue is against the back of the bottom teeth, and your throat is not constricted in any way. You must let your diaphragm do the hard work!

- Go for a loud, open tone. Work on sustaining long notes until they resonate in your chest. You are aiming for a non-shaky sound. If your voice shakes on a note, go down to a lower note and try again.

- Singing in chest voice is hard work. If you get tired, stop and come back to it again tomorrow. It's ok to take a break.

Chest Voice Placement Exercises

Here are two specific techniques that are helpful in getting you to achieve the correct placement and tone when you are singing in chest voice. The first I like to call "The Bull's Eye." When you are about to sing a phrase and you want to project the sound using your chest voice, look for a nearby wall or window. Imagine a bull's eye on that wall or window and pretend the phrase you are singing is an arrow shooting straight at the target. This kind of mental imagery helps those difficult phrases you sing come out strong, loud, resonant, and without restraint to the vocal cords. Best of all, you can practice this technique in any circumstance, whether you're at home running through a song, or if you're standing in front of any size audience and you need a mental reminder of correct tone placement.

One other technique works especially well for the placement of chest voice phrases. Many times if you are singing in chest voice for an extended period, it's easy to sit on the pitches and cause them to go flat. For this technique, take a particular phrase that you are having difficulty on and sing the pitched notes and rhythm by using the bubble hum. A bubble hum is like blowing a "raspberry" with your lips but putting it to a pitch. If you have trouble sustaining the bubble hum, you can gently hold both sides of your mouth with your fingertips. After you have practiced the bubble hum several times, use the same phrase, but sing the notes and rhythm using the buzz hum. Make sure your buzz hum feels hollow. Your lips should be closed, but your mouth and articulators should feel wide open inside. After you've repeated the phrase on the buzz hum several times, go back and sing the same phrase with the original words. Notice how this technique helps you get right on the pitch, because you practiced it with correct technique and placement of sound.

The key to developing a powerful chest voice is to let your diaphragm do the hard work. If you are singing and belting correctly, there should never be any strain to the throat. You may get tired after singing in chest voice for an extended period, but you shouldn't feel any discomfort. I've saved the best news for last: it's easier to learn to correctly engage the diaphragm in your chest voice than the other registers, because low notes tend to come more naturally. So, start practicing these tips today, and you'll be amazed at the power that emerges from your voice when used correctly!

Singer's Next Steps

- Work through some vocal exercises specifically designed to strengthen the chest register this week. See how long you can hold a low tone with correct placement and with as much power as possible.

- When practicing your own material, utilize the bull's eye technique and the humming techniques presented in this chapter. Both of these are great for refocusing the sound and helping you move through difficult phrases.

- Make sure that you feel your stomach (diaphragm) working every time you sing. It should start to be a habit at this point.

Week Six: Singing in the Sweet Spot— the Mixed Voice

Think of your mixed voice as your secret weapon in singing! If you have increased your head range and worked hard on strengthening your chest voice, the next step is to work on the mixed voice. For women, the mixed range is a combination of the chest and head ranges. For men, it is a combination of the head voice and falsetto. It's very difficult and harmful to try to sing in your chest range all the time. And it's not very powerful to use head voice, unless you've been classically trained to do so. Using your mixed voice when performing will prolong a healthy voice. When you are performing with a microphone, using your mixed voice will allow you to project appropriately without screaming, but with the beautiful sweetness of the head voice.

Roger Kain (author of *The Complete Vocal Workout*) says, "The mixed head voice is the most valuable of all the voices available to you. It can turn a good singer into a great one, because it allows you to choose and control your sounds."[6] However, the mixed voice is often the hardest voice to find. It's easier to feel the resonance in different areas of the body when singing in the chest and head ranges. I've read research that suggests it may take an adult several months to years to develop mixed range, if he or she has had no prior training. Once you find it, it is well worth the effort that it takes to develop, because being able to mix the voice hides breaks in your range and proves that you have developed control over your total singing range.

Unfortunately, there seems to be a lack of quality research on how to properly develop the mixed voice, so I will share with you my personal experience using my mixed range.

I have been singing in church since I was three years old, so naturally I became accustomed to using a microphone from a young age. In my experience, using a microphone often is one of the easiest ways to develop the mixed range. That is because the microphone amplifies the voice without much effort on the singer's part. When I want to sing stronger notes in the chest range, I don't have to push as hard as when I'm singing without a microphone. And on the higher head range notes, I can add just a little more breath support and the sound will be full, rich, and high! This is the way I was naturally able to develop my mixed voice without realizing what I was doing. I am very comfortable using it today. I almost feel more comfortable using my mixed voice than my chest or head voice because I have used it successfully most of my life. When I went to music school, I suddenly faced a new dilemma when I had to sing in classrooms with no microphones. It was then that I became aware of the importance of developing strong chest and head ranges so I could project naturally. The majority of the time in rehearsals and performances, I use my mixed voice. This allows me to maintain flexibility in range hour after hour; and I believe it's the reason why I rarely get hoarse, unless I'm coming down with an illness.

The mixed voice has been called the "magic, velvet" range. When used from bottom to top, it truly gives the impression that you have no breaks in your voice. Many people we consider to be professional singers have the ability to use their mixed voice to cover any discrepancies in their ranges. Therefore, one of the quickest ways to be viewed as a professional in the world of singing is to work hard on developing that mixed range. It truly makes you a versatile singer.

Now we come to the question: how exactly do you develop your mixed range? As I said before, it may be the hardest voice to find, because we don't seem to have as many physical indicators that we're singing in mixed voice, such as we do in chest voice or head voice. Singing in chest voice seems to be laborious work, with deep resonance below the head. Singing in head voice can sometimes feel light and airy, depending on how you approach different high notes. Singing in mixed voice should feel like a cross between the two. You should have the power of the chest voice (without actually singing full voice), with the agility and lightness of the head voice. Once you find the proper placement of the mixed voice, it should not be a struggle to sing in, because it is formed in the sinuses.

When working to develop the mixed range, it's definitely helpful to get behind a microphone any time you get the chance. Then once you're singing, adjust your voice accordingly. If you hear your voice coming out of the speakers too loudly, pull the sound back. If you're too soft, take a deep breath and push more air out to increase your volume without screaming. Learning how to properly sing with a microphone will aid in developing a strong mixed voice.

Here is a good method to help you work on your mixed voice: In your practice time, choose a song that contains notes mostly in the middle of your range. You don't want a song that is too high or too low. Listen to the singer as he or she demonstrates it, and then using the techniques you've learned for developing your head and chest range, begin to learn a section of the song. By the time you've completed this exercise, you will have sung through the section at least three different times. Start by singing the section in your head voice. Keep the tone light and visualize the sound coming from your forehead. Because the song is not high, this may be difficult at first, but keep trying until you are certain you can sing the entire passage in your head voice.

Now, perform a chest voice warm-up and perform the same section of song entirely in your chest voice. You want the resonance to feel as if it is coming from your chest. Be sure to use your diaphragm as you sing, and you should only sing the passage through once in your chest voice, especially if it's not as developed yet as the head voice. Once you've sung the passage in chest voice, aim to sing the passage in a healthy mix of both head and chest voice. You don't want too much air, nor do you want the section to feel or sound too heavy. Aim for a healthy mix of both. Keep working with the section of the song this week in your mixed voice and you will notice that this part of your range will gradually feel more comfortable as you get to the end of week. If you're up for the challenge, finish learning the rest of song, being sure to perform it in your mixed range.

If you're having trouble finding your mixed voice, it may be as simple as spending more time working through chest and head voices. Just remember, all the ranges are interconnected so strengthening one range will help them all. Once you feel that your chest and head ranges are opening up, begin to work through exercises that cover all parts of your range, from bottom to top and from top to bottom. Your long-term goal should be to sing through exercises without the voice breaking through the passagio.

Once you have developed the mixed voice, you will be surprised at the gains you make in your full range, and you will notice that you can sing for increasing periods without extreme fatigue to your voice. Your tone will improve and be consistently smooth over high, mid, and low notes. The mixed range really is the sweet spot in your voice!

Practice it often and use it to its full capacity when performing.

Singer's Next Steps

- Have a voice instructor take you through a simple scale and make note of where your voice breaks. It should be close to the Ab note above middle C (for women). This is the area where your chest changes to head voice and where you should take full advantage of using mixed voice.

- Sing a simple song with a microphone and utilize the techniques presented in this chapter to control your amplified sound. Yes, I am giving you an excuse to go sing karaoke! Just stay away from the secondhand smoke!

- Practice vocal exercises starting at the top of your range and ending at the bottom of your range and attempt to keep the same volume and smooth tone the entire way down. Be careful that your voice doesn't "break" when transitioning from head to chest ranges. If it does break, try the exercise a few more times to smooth out your ranges and successfully integrate your newfound mixed range.

Week Seven: Emotions in Singing

As a singer and performer, it's important that you realize that singing technically correct is just the beginning. You have to first master the mechanics of singing: voice registers, singing from the diaphragm, and creating resonance (what we've just spent the last month and a half working through) so you can concentrate on conveying appropriate emotion with each song you sing. There is nothing in this world like the feeling of captivating an audience through a compelling, emotional song.

Emotion in singing is what makes watching musicals so engaging. Not only are professional singers exercising their mastery of vocal technique, they are also able to pour their hearts out on stage. It's those emotions that come through their music that make the audience believe the storyline is actually taking place in that theater. A cast member might have an incredible voice, but if he or she displayed no emotion behind the music being sung, the audience would quickly get bored and lose interest.

The bottom line is this:

Boring singers are uncomfortable to watch, and overly animated singers are embarrassing to watch.

You must inject appropriate emotion into your singing every time you perform. If you are just standing there, you give the audience the illusion that you don't really care for what you are singing and that you can't wait to finish the song. If, on the other hand, you are moving all over the stage, making ridiculous hand motions, you come across as trying too hard to move the audience, and you're more than likely to elicit a few covered laughs behind your audience's hands.

Emotion in singing is so important, because it sells the message you are trying to convey. It makes the music come alive and touches the audience. The emotion must always match the song. You wouldn't paste on a big cheesy smile while singing a somber break-up song. Likewise, you don't want to give off the impression that you are being tortured while you sing a song about being victorious. I know this sounds like common sense, but you'd be surprised at the number of performers whose lack of emotion in their music makes me think they want to be doing anything else but singing!

When you want to inject emotion into your singing, you have to first know what emotion(s) you're going to portray. What I recommend is to pull out the lyric sheet of the most recent song you've been practicing and read it aloud, much like you would recite a poem. Highlight or underline your favorite lines or those power phrases that seem to comprise the main message of the song. Now go back and think about words that describe the meaning of the song. List them in bold print at the top of the lyric sheet. For example, recently I was working with one of my younger students on the song "Do-Re-Mi" from the iconic musical, *The Sound of Music.* When we were talking about the words that describe this song, we came up with whimsical, teachable, and happy. Those were the emotions I told her to try to portray when she was singing "Do-Re-Mi." Now you try it with a song you are working on. For each song you perform, you should have a few different emotion words. If you're doing three songs that all portray the same emotion, replace one or two with songs that have different emotions!

I just had the privilege of recording an upbeat children's song this week. On my lyric sheet in the recording studio, I wrote emotion words such as informative, happy-go-lucky, and Disney-like. When I recorded the song, I was in a room by myself, but I still tried to inject as much of those emotion words in my singing as I could. The result is that the audio of my voice on that song came out sounding exactly as I wanted with the appropriate emotion coming through.

Once you have determined some emotion words to your song, now the challenge is communicating those emotions. Here are some ways that we communicate emotions when singing:

- **Words and phrasing:** certain words or phrases demand more emotion than others do. For instance, "I'm desperate for you" would not and should not be sung the same way as "I hope you visit." Using different vocal colors and techniques in phrasing can be an effective technique of portraying emotion.

- **Dynamics:** soft and loud singing can communicate emotions. If you are belting a phrase and suddenly drop the volume on the next line, you are immediately grabbing the audience's attention. Every song you sing should include some dynamics. On your lyric sheet, it is often helpful to document where you want the dynamics to go and then work on incorporating them into the song each time you practice.

- **Tone:** bright, mellow, warm, smooth. Most of us have a tone we use the majority of the time, but it is possible to change your tone to meet the emotional content of a song. One example is when you warm your tone up to sing a jazz ballad.

- **Beat and tempo:** this largely has to do with the accompaniment of a song, however, singers sometimes open songs with a slow chorus to "invite" the audience in, before launching into the true, more upbeat tempo of the song. You don't have control over this if you are using a pre-recorded track, but if you perform with live musicians, you can experiment with the beat and tempo to see how drastically this can affect the emotion of a song.

- **Facial expression:** Wow, is this one important! If you're singing a happy song, please don't show the audience a face that suggests you're having a tooth pulled! It's fine to smile when you're singing, as long as it doesn't get in the way of good vocal technique! Have a good time when you sing, and let it show through your face. Sing with your eyes!

- **Body motions:** The body is an effective tool to use in portraying emotion, as long as it's used the right way. Tapping a foot, raising a hand, or gently swaying the body can all be appropriate ways of conveying emotion in songs.

If you're someone who has a hard time portraying emotion when you sing, be encouraged because you can practice and improve. There are several highly effective ways to practice emotion and inject more (or less if need be) into your music. The first one I've already touched on, and that is to determine the appropriate emotion(s) of the song and list them on your lyric sheet. You have to know what you want to portray to the audience. Next, practice your song in a full-length mirror, if possible. Watch yourself throughout the whole song. Make notes of what seems natural and what seems forced. If you're not used to using your hands, incorporate some hand movements into the song and see exactly what it looks like. Pay attention to your face. Are you smiling enough? Too much? Are you raising your eyebrows every time you sing a high note? The key here is to really learn what you look like when you sing, and figure out which emotions look most natural and convey your interest in the song. You want to see what your audience sees when you're performing.

It's also extremely helpful to make an audio recording of yourself singing. You don't need fancy equipment; any digital recorder will do, and many smart phones have recording capability. Sing through a song while recording it, then listen through it and ask yourself if you can hear the emotion. Now, go back through and record the same song but this time, sing it as full of emotion as possible. Make it over the top. Use hand gestures, foot taps, and whatever else helps you to be full of emotion. Listen to that recording, and you'll probably hear a huge difference from the first one.

Finally, for those of you who are brave enough to try this: have someone film you singing. A visual of your performance can greatly aid in helping you improve your craft. Watch the video and look objectively at the emotions you're portraying. Are you coming across as genuine, or could you use more emotion in your singing? Are your hand and body moments too much, too little, or just right? What about your stance? Do you come across as comfortable while singing?

Emotion is an important aspect of singing and one that can be conveyed in so many different ways. The key is to always gauge your emotions when you're singing, make improvements, and always keep learning.

Singer's Next Steps

- Take a current song you are rehearsing and make a list of emotion words on the top of your lyric sheet. Incorporate these emotions into your daily practice.

- Record yourself singing your song using both of the ways described in this chapter. Listen to both and see if you notice a difference between the recordings.
- Sing your entire selection while watching yourself in the mirror.

Week Eight: Dealing with Performance Anxiety

Sweaty palms, shallow breathing, butterflies in your stomach, the urge to use the bathroom when you don't have to—all of these are common examples of nervousness you may experience before singing. I say before, because for many singers, these symptoms decrease or go away altogether once they get into the song. Other singers continue to experience nerves throughout the entire performance, which can be debilitating to both confidence and proper tone.

On one hand, nervousness can completely wreck a performance. You may have practiced it one way, but then you have to sing it in front of someone, and it comes out completely different. You think, "That's not really my voice! I know I'm better than that!" In this case, nerves have taken over and kept you from performing your best and really enjoying the sensation that singing brings.

On the other hand, a healthy case of nerves can give you the adrenaline rush you need to step out on a stage and own the song you're about to sing. If you are able to push through the nerves and concentrate on the experience of singing, nervousness can actually aid in helping you achieve that "singer's high," which is one of the most rewarding experiences for singers. In that moment, you feel as if there is nothing you would rather be doing than singing. All your notes are "in the pocket" and your voice comes across as effortless to the audience.

Nerves are a part of singing, and I've yet to meet a singer (professional or amateur) who doesn't get nervous before a performance. Only you know if your nerves aid you or deter you from giving your best performance. For most of us, nervousness is a nuisance, and we allow it to get in the way of singing with our best voice. However, there are ways to effectively channel nerves into a positive aid in performing. The first step is to remember that nervousness is natural and every singer deals with it. I have been performing since I could walk, and I'd love to say I no longer feel nervousness before singing, but that would not be true. I personally don't believe any singer who says they never get nervous. If that's really true, then I have to question their humility. Once you get to the point that you think you've arrived, learned everything there is to know, and you're better than everybody else is, you're probably in for a rude awakening!

Which brings me to an important point: many times nerves are caused by our insecurities about what others might be thinking about our voice, song, and performance. Part of a pleasant performing experience is taking the stage with confidence that you have what it takes to sing the song you've worked hard to prepare! You are original, and you have a unique voice that no one else possesses. It's fine to emulate singers and copy vocal techniques that you like, but recognize that you won't ever completely sound like someone else; neither will anyone ever sound exactly like you. That's a good thing! Think of how boring it would be if ten different people sang the same song the exact same way. Variety is the spice of life, and your voice can do something that someone else's voice may not be able to do. So embrace your voice and own it! God gave it to you for a reason.

Aside from gaining confidence, another surefire way to combat nerves is to always be prepared. If you get up to sing and have no idea what the first phrase is, then yes, you probably will be nervous, and rightfully so! Chances are you haven't taken the time to properly prepare for the performance.

You need to practice singing on a regular basis (and I shouldn't have to remind you about this in week eight)! One of the easiest and effortless ways to learn your music is to listen to it repeatedly in the car. Got a thirty-minute commute on the way to work in the morning? Put the song you're working through on repeat and practice it from your driveway all the way to your job. By the time you get there, you'll have a good start at memorizing it and getting the song stuck in your head, which is a good thing when you're trying to learn music quickly. Your ultimate goal is to get the lyrics and pitches so engrained in your head that you don't have to think about them when you get up to sing. You'll just be able to perform and concentrate on the emotions of the song.

A helpful practice to employ in all areas of your life, not just in singing, is the practice of positive visualization. This technique is used a lot in sports training, but it's also effective for any areas of your life that need a confidence boost. Close your eyes and mentally see yourself performing. Place yourself in the exact environment where you will be performing and run through the whole song in your head. Watch yourself hitting every note, displaying the proper emotions, and doing your personal best. Never visualize yourself making mistakes, but always see yourself as succeeding. If you happen to mess up in your mental performance, start it over again in your mind and see yourself as completely successful. Your subconscious cannot tell the difference between reality and dreams, so if you constantly see yourself performing at your best, your brain interprets that as real and does everything to set you up for that real-life outcome.

Probably the most effective technique in combating nerves is recognizing that God is on your side. God promised in the scriptures that he would be with us, even unto the end of the age

(Matthew 28:20). But how often do we walk around unaware of his presence in our daily lives? He's offered us his help for everything we face, but so often we try to take on the weight of the world by ourselves. If you are singing for God, why not allow his presence to afford you the peace you need when performing? Recognize that his power and ability within you is there to strengthen you and get the message out that so many hurting people need to hear.

My absolute favorite scripture on the subject of stage fright comes from 2 Timothy 1:7:[7] "For God hath not given us the spirit of fear; but of power, and of love, and of a sound mind." Recognize that the message you seek to convey through your singing is a message that has the power to convict and the love to heal. If God's word promises you a sound mind, then all you have to do is claim it and walk around with the confidence that you are his child and he has empowered you to sing your song.

Singer's Next Steps

- Find your scripture for singing. It could be either one mentioned above or maybe you have another meaningful promise. Memorize it and meditate on it before every performance.

- Before your next performance, take some time daily the week before to visualize yourself singing with ease and confidence.

- Make sure you are properly prepared for each performance. Ideally, you should be able to sing a song in your sleep before stepping out on a stage to sing it in front of an audience. Remember, being completely prepared is a great way to combat nervous energy!

- Do you have other favorite ways of dealing with nervousness? If they work for you, be sure to employ them before every performance.

Week Nine: Dealing with Common Vocal Problems

To maintain an optimal singing voice, you should be familiar with common voice problems and know how to treat them. Ignoring a not-so-serious vocal problem now could cause you more harmful issues later. So, do all you can to care for your instrument. If it breaks, you can't just go out and purchase another one!

Your voice is the only one you have, so treat it with the respect and the care that it deserves!

When I was earning my bachelor's degree in vocal performance, all voice students had end-of-the-semester performances called juries. In these highly stressful performances, each student had to perform multiple songs in front of a panel of professors. Not only did the professors get to choose which songs the singer would sing in the performance, but also a huge portion of the semester grade was based on that single performance! Talk about nerve-racking!

Here's the funny part: I used to always get sick right before those performances and come down with a major case of laryngitis, so my jury often had to be moved to the beginning of the following semester. This happened several times for me, and I never knew why. I wasn't trying to get sick and lose my voice. It just seemed to naturally happen right around jury time. Now I look back and realize that I felt so much stress riding on that one event every semester that my voice reacted to it by becoming hoarse. I don't think we have any idea just how much harm stress can cause our bodies, but I truly believe (because I've experienced it firsthand) that it can affect the voice in a major way.

If you find yourself stressed out, don't be surprised if you're not singing at your peak level. Take some time for yourself and relax. Do what makes you happy, and see if it doesn't change the outlook on the rest of your day. If you're able to, take a break from singing and come back renewed and refreshed the next day. There's no point in getting frustrated about your voice when you're stressed out about something else in your life. Try as much as possible to eliminate unnecessary stress in your life, and your singing will ultimately benefit.

A common issue many singers face is getting sore throats after singing. The most obvious cause for this may be that a singer is letting the throat handle all the stress of the notes, thus causing tenderness or soreness. In this case, the singer needs to stop singing as soon as possible, give the voice a rest, and resume singing when he/she is making sure the diaphragm is fully engaged. Remember that proper singing should never hurt!

Do not do further damage to your instrument by trying to "push through" a difficult song if your throat is bothering you. Take a break as soon as you can, and even more important, make sure you are engaging the diaphragm each time you sing. It may be a good time to take a break from singing and review some breathing exercises to ensure that you are fully connecting the breath to the diaphragm. Then you can return to light singing when your throat is no longer sore.

Another possible reason for a sore throat is if the singer is coming down with a cold. Many times, an infection may start with a sore throat, move to the sinuses, and finish off in the chest. If you sense you are getting sick, drink as much water as you can, take your vitamins, and get some rest. These preventative measures may keep you from getting sick, or at least shorten a cold's duration.

Many singers also complain of experiencing hoarseness after long periods of singing. I have to question whether or not they are using the correct methods of singing, such as engaging the diaphragm, expanding the ribs, or using proper breath support. Once again, not supporting the sound by using the entire body can place unnecessary strain on the throat and articulators and cause immediate fatigue. Hoarseness is the voice's way of saying, "Stop using me the wrong way!" Remember that singing is a full-body experience. Support the sound all the way from the bottom of the feet and let it extend up through the mouth with ease. If you do experience hoarseness, there is little that you can do to immediately clear it up. Don't try to force your voice to sing through it. This can do extreme damage! Let the voice rest, and once you do begin singing again, make sure to warm-up well.

I've come across many singers who are "missing" part of their ranges, whether it is lower, middle, or high. Basically, I will take a singer through a scale and certain notes will sound like a whisper or croak when the singer gets to them. There are many different reasons why this happens. One could be that the singer has not done enough work to expand weak parts of the range, whether it be chest, mix, or head voice. In addition, incorrectly shaping the words or vowel sounds can restrict the full, resonant sound that singers should strive to achieve. If a singer doesn't use enough breath, the sound may not have enough power behind it to sound full. In the case of missing ranges, I recommend working through mixed voice exercises to eliminate the breaks in the voice, and allow all the pitches to flow at the same level of intensity.

If you are a singer who experiences tone problems, as in your tone is not clear or strong or resonant, you should make sure you are breathing deeply when you sing, aim to shoot the sound out toward an imaginary target, and make sure you are enunciating your words. Many singers who have a muffled tone just need to change the way they are shaping their words with the articulators, and the sound of the voice will become clearer on its own. If you don't know how to describe your tone, record yourself singing and ask another singer to listen and give you a fair assessment of your tone. Then you can work to correct any issues you may experience and learn to project a clear, vibrant tone.

Another common problem is the lack of flexibility in the voice. This means that it's hard to perform a series of notes quickly and clearly. The voice may get "stuck" on one note or slow down in an attempt to sing all the notes involved in a passage. To improve your flexibility, use vocal exercises that have descending and ascending scales and move quickly. You can start slow at first, but gradually increase your speed and focus on the quality of each quick note.

One last thing to mention while we're discussing vocal care: if you are about to sing for a long period, it's best to refrain from taking a pain reliever. Pain pills block the body's pain receptors; however, they can also cause a singer to over-sing, because the singer can't as easily gauge discomfort in the cords. If needed, wait to take a pain reliever until after you sing.

Sometimes, the voice needs rest. Don't always talk if you don't have to. Use warm-ups methodically. Drink water and take care of the rest of your body through stress management and exercise. Care for your voice, and it is sure to serve you well the rest of your life.

Lubricating the Voice

How many of us are actually getting the recommended amount of water into our bodies every day? Probably a much smaller percentage than we can imagine. This is an area that even I struggle to maintain. After a while, I just get tired of chugging water! But, it is the best way to lubricate the voice and keep the body hydrated. Singer or not, all people need water. And most of us could stand to up our daily intake.

There are some sneaky ways to increase your water intake. Recently on the market, reusable water bottles with built-in filters have popped up. I received one as a Christmas gift and found that I seemed to drink more water throughout the day if I just kept the bottle with me as I taught lessons and music classes. Another sneaky way of getting more water is to stick a straw in your drink. For some reason, it seems easier to drink more this way.

Finally, if you are really struggling with your intake, start recording the approximate number of ounces you do drink per day and aim to add 8 ounces (or the equivalent of one cup) to that number each day. By the end of the week, you should be close to the recommended 64 ounces. If you are a person who enjoys a soda with lunch or dinner, aim to replace half of the soda with water. Then you have the best of both worlds, but you're still getting some water intake.

If you are like me and enjoy a nice cup of coffee, try to limit your caffeine intake on days that you will be singing. For instance, I've made it a rule that I don't have coffee on Sundays. I know I will be singing for several hours at a time, and coffee does not serve my voice well when I have to perform. Therefore, I have decaffeinated tea with a little honey if I feel like a flavored beverage; otherwise, I stick to water. On days when I do drink coffee, I try to match the ounces of coffee that I drink with water to avoid dehydration.

The bottom line is that water must be replenished daily to keep your body functioning optimally, and it is simply the best way to hydrate if you want healthy vocal cords.

Singer's Next Steps

- What kind of vocal problems do you deal with, and how will you treat them after reading through this chapter?

- Track your water intake for a week. Create a list of the amounts that you drink. Make adjustments if you need to increase your intake. Notice how this improves your singing voice or your overall health. Your body will thank you!

Week Ten: Finding Your Performing Niche

Congratulations! If you've found yourself at the last chapter of this book, I'm assuming you have spent the last two-and-a-half months working to improve your voice. Think of how much more you now know about your instrument and how this information will enable you to be successful for the rest of your singing career! You should be extremely proud of yourself for taking the time to improve your singing. I hope you are already feeling and hearing the difference in your range, tone, and breathing.

Before you break open a bottle of bubbly (aka, sparkling water, that is!), consider what you want to do with your newfound knowledge of singing. Maybe you already have a place to sing for people or maybe your extent of performing has been limited to the shower. Either way, now is the time to show off your newly acquired skills. It's time to start thinking about where you might be able to do so.

Rock Star Status Not Included

I wish I could include a surefire way to get every person who reads and works through this vocal book a performance. Unfortunately, just because you have the skills to sing better doesn't mean you'll ever get to use them, unless you get out into the world and find your own performance opportunities. But here's the beauty in your choosing: you know where you will be comfortable performing and where you wouldn't dare go. The choice is yours, but for the last week of our vocal training, your assignment is to scope out some performance venues where you can practice your craft. Who knows what kind of possibility you might open up for yourself in the process!

Having a hard time coming up with ideas? Use the following as a jumping-off point.

- **Family reunion:** What's so great about singing at your family reunion? Well, you're guaranteed that Aunt Bertha's going to enjoy your performance, even if she left her hearing aid at home. One note of caution though—sometimes it's hardest to sing in front of family and friends or people who know you the best. If you struggle with self-confidence, you might want to pick a starting venue with a few more strangers. That way you don't feel like everyone in the room is judging you.
- **Nursing and retirement homes:** If you've never had the opportunity to sing in a senior home, this could be the best possible venue to start with. Many senior

homes struggle to find entertainment and end up resorting to the same performers week after week. The residents always appreciate a newcomer taking the time to entertain them. And most old folks will enjoy any type of music (besides heavy metal) that you'd like to present them. Reggae, jazz, pop, oldies, and hymns: it doesn't really matter. You're bringing some joy to your audience and logging great practice in the meantime. Simply call up or, better yet, pay a visit to the home closest to you and ask to speak with the activities director. He or she will be able to tell you what they are looking for and how soon you might be able to perform.

- **Local restaurants:** Gigs in local restaurants do exist, and many of them have the added bonus of providing you with monetary tips, but I don't recommend searching out these venues unless you have some previous experience. Obviously, you'll need to have accompaniment, whether you play piano or guitar yourself or hire out musicians. And you'll need an extensive set list, probably about 15–20 songs that you feel comfortable performing in a single evening. Even if you're not ready to start performing in a local restaurant, it could be a goal to work up to while you're practicing and learning new material each week. Eventually, it could turn out to be a sweet (paid) deal!

- **Community events:** It doesn't matter where you live. Somewhere close to you is a community event that could possibly provide you with a performance opportunity. To get started, browse through your local paper or online to find the Calendar of Events. Some events listed may already have booked entertainment, but you could always offer to step in as a back-up performer if someone has to drop out last minute. Community events are a great way to get started in the performance world and begin to network with others who love to do what you do.

- **Join a show:** In the Calendar of Events, you might find opportunities to audition for different shows in your area. Whether you're looking for a classical choir or a hit musical, there are usually multiple opportunities for you to indulge in your genre. Be sure to get the specifics about each show you are auditioning for and please go in prepared! You will probably need a headshot photograph and a resume, but even if you're just beginning, you will most likely be granted an audition. And even if you don't make a show, an audition is a fantastic learning experience. Once you have one under your belt, it's much easier to add to it. Likewise, once you have performed in one show, you have experience to add to your resume, which is most helpful in procuring more music opportunities.

- **Church:** One of my favorite performance venues is the local church. I'm somewhat biased because I have literally grown up performing in churches, but I can also say without a doubt, most of my singing opportunities have been born out of performing in places of worship. If you are not keen on singing solos, perhaps your church has a choir. Most church choirs will welcome new members. You can gain friends and great singing experience by joining a church choir. And when the time is right, you can probably even audition for a solo performance. Many churches have special events built into their music program, especially around Easter and Christmas. These are great opportunities to get involved and just might hook you into coming back for more.

- **Recitals:** If you decide to study with a voice teacher, ask him or her if they offer student recitals. Many vocal coaches will hold recitals to showcase their students' progress. Family and friends have a chance to hear you also. If none of the other options works, perhaps a recital is a great first choice, if your voice teacher offers it.

No matter where you live, there is a performance opportunity available to you, if you'll only take the time to seek it out. I hope the list above gives you some great ideas on how to get started.

Showcasing Your Skills as a Professional

One of my favorite sayings is "success begets success," meaning once you've done something successfully, there is a good chance you'll have more opportunities to duplicate that success. I have found this to be true in the field of entertainment and every other area of my life.

However, one of the easiest ways to ensure you are successful is to always present yourself as a professional. Whether singing is your career or simply a hobby, people are impressed by a go-getter who is constantly preparing new material and trying out new skills. In the coming weeks as you seek out singing opportunities, strive to put your best foot forward to everyone you meet. When you go to an audition or a meeting, dress professionally. Carry your material in a clean folder or binder and always be prepared to sing on the spot if asked. In fact, it's probably a great idea to go to any music-related meeting warmed-up so you can easily jump into singing your performance material.

The bottom line is this—people are going to naturally gravitate toward the prepared, professional individual over someone who comes in ten minutes late, slovenly dressed, and forgets words or is not prepared to sing. Whether or not you are being paid to sing, start telling yourself you are a professional musician and project that image to everyone you meet. You never know what opportunities may come of it!

Living and Learning

If you've stuck with me throughout this small book, I hope you've heard and felt incredible and exciting growth in your voice during the last two-and-a-half months. I hope you've gained confidence to perform and showcase your skills. This book is just the beginning of all there is to learn about singing. Every voice is different; that's why the art of singing is not an exact science. If a method is not working for you, don't be afraid to try something new. If a vocal exercise leaves you feeling strained and tired, throw it out and find another. It's your voice and your life. You hold the reins. You can go as far as you want with your music. The key is to never stop searching and never stop learning. There is always something you can work on to improve, whether it is more control over breath support or managing stage fright.

Once you've finished the steps in this book, you may want to start it over. If you've made this much progress in ten weeks, think of the progress you can make in another ten!

Remember, your voice is your instrument. It's the only one you have, so you owe it to yourself to take care of it in the best possible way every day.

A Note about Performing

Self-evaluation is extremely important in performances. That is why I have included a blank self-evaluation form that you can print out or copy and use each time you perform, whether it is in front of others or just by yourself.

You need to be able to view your performances through a neutral eye. The unfortunate truth is that most of us are harder on ourselves than others are. We are quick to point out every little thing we've done wrong, and we are not as fast to compliment ourselves on the things we did well. I want you to take some time and figure out where you've improved in the past ten weeks, and also determine what still needs work. You should be able to give yourself constructive criticism without demolishing your self-esteem.

In the performance setting, your peers will also have the opportunity to give constructive feedback. Listen to what they are saying, but if you don't agree with something, don't let it keep you from performing. We are all seeking to become better vocalists, and part of that process involves hearing what others think of your singing.

After reading and implementing the strategies in this book, I hope that you are just a little more comfortable standing in front of an audience and performing a song. I know you have already made huge strides in improving your vocal technique and will continue to do so as long as you make time to practice the techniques presented to you in this book.

I am proud of you and hope you are proud of yourself for all you've accomplished!

Self-Evaluation for a Musical Performance

Make a copy of this page for every time you complete and perform a new song.

Date of performance:

Song you are performing:

Artist who sings this song:

On a scale of 1–5 rate your level of nervousness before performing
(1 being not nervous at all, 3 being neutral, 5 being petrified):

1   2   3   4   5

Fill out this section after the performance.

What did you find easy to sing about this song?

What did you find difficult to sing about this song?

What voice range did you primarily use in this song (chest, mix, or head)?

What did you do well?

What do you think could use improvement?

About the Author

Kristin King has been singing and performing since the tender age of three, when she sang her first solo, "Row, Row, Row Your Boat" in church. She resides in Port Orange, Florida, where she runs a successful music studio from her home, teaching voice lessons and piano lessons. She graduated from Belmont University with a bachelor of music degree in vocal performance. When she is not advocating for proper vocal health, she is performing, directing a church choir rehearsal, or teaching elementary music. Kristin resides with her husband, Jamie; Yorkshire terrier, Bella; and the newest singer in the family, son Landon Christopher.

For more information on Kristin's vocal techniques, check out her blog at www.thechoirsinger.blogspot.com. She can also be reached by email at jandkking@yahoo.com.

Endnotes

1. See <u>Home | NYU Voice Center | NYU Langone Medical Center | New York, NY</u>. Accessed January 21, 2014.
2. Roger Kain, *The Complete Vocal Workout: A Step-By-Step Guide to Tough Vocals* (Music Sales America, 2006), 13.
3. Anne Peckham, *Vocal Workouts for the Contemporary Singer* (Boston: Berklee Press, 2005), 37.
4. Holy Bible, New International Version® NIV®, 2011, Biblica, Inc.
5. See "Chest Voice," <u>http://foreversinging.com/archives/2010/03/chest-voice/</u>. Accessed January 22, 2014.
6. Kain, *The Complete Vocal Workout,* 71.
7. Holy Bible, King James Version, 1604, public domain.

69769523R00071

Made in the USA
Columbia, SC
22 April 2017